Setting the World in Order

Previous Walt McDonald First-Book Winners

Heartwood, Miriam Vermilya
Into a Thousand Mouths, Janice Whittington
A Desk in the Elephant House, Cathryn Essinger
Stalking Joy, Margaret Benbow
An Animal of the Sixth Day, Laura Fargas
Anna and the Steel Mill, Deborah Burnham
The Andrew Poems, Shelly Wagner
Between Towns, Laurie Kutchins
The Love That Ended Yesterday in Texas, Cathy Smith Bowers

Setting the World in Order

Rick Campbell

Texas Tech University Press

This book was set in Adobe Garamond and Goudy Oldstyle. The paper used in this book meets the minimum requirements of ANSI/NISO Z39.48-1992 (R1997). ⊗

Printed in the United States of America

Design by Bryce Burton

Library of Congress Cataloging-in-Publication Data
    Campbell, Rick.
        Setting the world in order : poems / by Rick Campbell.
            p. cm. — (The Walt McDonald first-book poetry series)
        ISBN 0-89672-447-6
            1. Pennsylvania—Poetry. 2. Voyages and travels—Poetry. I. Title.
    II. Series.
    PS3553.A487324 S48 2001
    811'.54—dc21
                                                    00-011805

    01 02 03 04 05 06 07 08 09 / 9 8 7 6 5 4 3 2 1

Texas Tech University Press
Box 41037
Lubbock, Texas 79409-1037 USA

1-800-832-4042

ttup@ttu.edu

http://www.ttup.ttu.edu

iv

for Marcia, Della Rose,
and Rosemary Campbell

The one tongue I can write in
Is my Ohioan
There most people are poor.
I thought I could not stand it
To go home anymore,
Yet I go home, every year . . .

James Wright

Acknowledgments

Grateful acknowledgment is made to the following
  publications in which some of these poems first
  appeared (often in different form):

Americas Review: "Body Song, Vietnam"
The Apalachee Quarterly: "Leaving Home, Pittsburgh
  1966," "Letter to Kathy from a Frigate at Sea"
Atlanta Review: "Pensacola Street Sunrise"
The Chattahoochee Review: "The Breathers, St. Mark's
  Lighthouse," "Orange Nights, Cold Stars"
Cottonwood: "Hanging Tobacco"
Crania: "Discourse," "Seashell Salesman"
The Devil's Millhopper: "Harmonica Lesson," "Well Done"
The Georgia Review: "How the Streets in Front of
  Kaufmann's Department Store Tell Me I Am Home,"
  "Legend," "Meditation on Today's Limit of Pleasure"
International Quarterly: "The Poem in the River"
Kalliope: "Proving Lake Okeechobee"
The Missouri Review: "Even the Ohio Can Change,"
  "Morrison's, 1968," "On Missing the First Step on the
  Moon," "Setting Pins," "The Spring in Tevebaugh
  Hollow," "To Jennifer, Thinking of Li Po"
Onionhead: "Fishing the Encampment" (as "The Bear")
The Panhandler: "Confluence" (as "A Grammar of
  Rivers"),"Ohio River Sunday"
Pig Iron: "Gasoline," (as "For the Valley")
Poet Lore: "Trying to Get Pregnant, Flying to Iowa,"
  "Caterpillars"
Prairie Schooner: "The Drowned Son"
Puerto Del Sol: "The History of Steel"
Q Magazine: "Juno Beach and the Sea Turtle"

The Quarterly Review: "Creeley Cursing in Church"
Red Cedar: "Seed Harvest," "A Walk in the Woods"
Rhino: "The Wall"
South Florida Poetry Review: "Horseshoe Crabs Mating at Carrabelle Beach"
The Snake Nation Review: "On the Water of My Mistakes"
Sundog: The Southeast Review: "Setting the World in Order"
Tar River Poetry: "The Geography of Desire"

"For the Old Men at the Grindstone Factory" appeared in *North of Wakulla*: *An Anhinga Anthology,* Anhinga Press, 1989. A number of these poems also appeared in *A Day's Work,* a State Street Press chapbook.

The author wishes to thank the Florida Arts Council, the Florida Division of Cultural Affairs, and the National Endowment for the Arts for grants that supported the writing of this book.

Contents

III

IV

V

Introduction

One of Robert Frost's most often quoted statements about love and poetry is that each of these adventures begins "in delight" and, with luck, ends "in wisdom"—"a clarification of life," "a momentary stay against confusion" ("The Figure a Poem Makes," *Modern Poetics*, 56). Teacher and fiction writer R. V. Cassill believes that the "whole spirit of writing is to overcome narrowness and fear by giving order, measure, and significance to the flux of experience constantly dinning into our lives" ("Author to Reader," *Writing Fiction*, 2nd ed., xv-xvi). The "act of writing," Cassill says, is "a way to possess your own life" ("Choosing a Subject," *Writing Fiction*, 2nd ed., 13).

The title of Rick Campbell's book of poems *Setting the World in Order* makes it clear from the outset that this collection is intended to be a unified, coherent quest to do just what the title boldly declares, to do what Frost and Cassill demand of good writing. These are personal poems, the speaker in the sequence almost the poet himself, and yet, as the poet/persona explains in "Discourse," the poems he likes best "seem to be / spoken by somebody else" who is and is not the poet, a person inside the poet's head, "a fleshy / full-bodied noun that I imagine / has to use doors like the rest of us." His is a "symbiotic life" that with luck and daring can lead to discovery and meaning.

Rick Campbell is a poet who expects the poetic process to bring order, bring clarification, meaning. His is not poetry "formed for arcane and uncertain / purpose" ("Discourse"). His poetic quest promises "to go somewhere," not leave us lost and "looking back at where we had been" ("Setting the World in Order"). A book structured around a quest for meaning, for order, does not, however, presuppose that the poet has already completed the journey and is now only showing slides of his adventure. The title is not *The World in Order. Setting* makes all the difference. This is an on-going process, a setting out, a voyage of discovery.

In *The Courage to Create*, psychologist Rollo May states that "to encounter 'the reality of experience' is surely the basis for all creativity" (26); the poet undertakes "the struggle to perceive and reproduce the world around him through his own vision of being human" (84). Rick Campbell's *Setting the World in Order* is the poet's personal odyssey leading from the Ohio River and Pennsylvania mill towns, from Pittsburgh to Florida by way of Wyoming and California, by way of James Wright's and Walt Whitman's America, as he seeks to escape a place he screams his hate for, but this hate "comes back love" ("The Poem in The River"), as he hungers for beauty, art, spiritual guidance, a home, a family, the waters of healing, his journey "to the springs of provenance" ("On the Water of My Mistakes") where he can at last claim ownership of a past that has led him to his destination, his new place of origin.

The book is organized into five sections, all very much place and people-centered, with the main locales being Ohio River mill towns, Pittsburgh, and Florida—places in the poet's geography of desire, his "cartography of the heart" ("The Geography of Desire"). The epigraph from James Wright initiates the book's quest motif, setting out from a home the poet thought he could not stand, implying the searcher's need to accept his old home, move on, and not dwell on a past, a place, already vanishing.

The epigraph leads into Part I's first two poems ("Legend" and "The Poem in the River") inviting the reader to join the poet on this quest, much like Walt Whitman invites the reader of "Song Of Myself" to assume what the poet assumes, joining him in singing the body and the soul of America. "Legend" identifies the poet as coming "from a land that didn't need words," a land he "left, crisscrossed / America." "Throughout his land he became legend," and no one "ever heard him speak. He saved it. / It's for you and you haven't come yet." Then "The Poem in the River" opens with the line "Someday you'll find this," reminiscent of the ending of "Song Of Myself"—"Failing to fetch me at first keep encouraged, / Missing me one place search another, / I stop somewhere waiting for you."

The first part of *Setting the World in Order* describes the land of the poet's fathers, the poet's heritage, as a rough, dangerous place: "If you leave here alive / your memory fades from their eyes" ("The Poem in the River"). It is a land of "the mill burning the black sky, cranking, screeching, hissing / through the night," but here is also the "beauty / of the fire and light dancing on slick water" ("The Poem in the River")—a paradox the poet is all too conscious of. He knows a "man's supposed to die / slow here. Forty years in the mill. Soot / in the attic settling in your lungs," and yet he acknowledges "the soot is our life; the river what we love" ("The Poem in the River"), again verbalizing the underlying paradox of his quest: "We know we were lucky / to be born here. Lucky / we learned to leave" ("Gasoline").

The poet's personal history begins in the Western Pennsylvania mill town of his youth, partially defined by "the drab brick walls / of St. John's church," his family church, the "tangible, . . . archeological smoothness of the cold, / rubbed pew," the "darkened and shined" wood of the communion rail where a boy could "kneel in the shiny indentations" ("Ohio River Sunday"). It is the 1960s, further defined for the poet by the assassination of President John Kennedy and by the Vietnam War and Larry W. Pierce "who fell trying to run the bases, / who could not hide in hide and seek," whose name is now melded "with fifty-thousand etched names" on the wall of The Vietnam Memorial ("The Wall").

For those who stay, death is often their way out, like Louie who fell "into the smelter and left / his strange mark on every beam / poured that week" ("Creely Cursing in Church"). For those who stay, their future will become the lives their fathers and grandfathers "believed in"—the life of the mills, the steel factories ("The Spring in Tevebaugh Hollow"). For the poet and his childhood friends, life was a pick-up game of baseball beside Tevebaugh Hollow's spring—"water sweeter than any borough pipes hauled." What they knew was that "life began there, at Tevebaugh, / when every last one of us was alive, / and the future hung like a slow curve." To connect with the fat seams of that future did not symbolize joining the line of their fathers; rather, it represented railroad tracks straight out of town; it meant driving their new lives deep into the "fence-less field" ("The Spring in Tevebaugh Hollow"). The poet, however, recognizes he can never fully leave behind this land of "abandoned mills / that were our daily bread"; he knows only too well "what earth rushes to claim me" ("The Candles at Margaret Mary Catholic Church").

Part One ends with the poet's acknowledging, "For years I have been lost," thinking he could sever his ties to his people, their voices singing "*Pittsburgh* when they say *Iron*," their heritage the past of "smoke / and ash of three shifts a day, whole valley working, / living mill lives" ("How The Streets in Front of Kaufmann's Department Store Tell Me I Am Home"). Now he knows he must confront his feelings about his past, his people—mill workers "together at last" standing on a downtown street "in front of Kaufmann's windows, waiting / for the light to change."

Part Two begins the poet's trek across America, a catalogue of the poet's work experiences. Through the nine poems in this section, the poet tracks his personal history of work as it often intersects with a regional and national history of people at work. As with Walt Whitman in "Song Of Myself," the poet is now *afoot with his vision:*

1966, the poet and his school friend Billy take a night job "setting pins in an alley / on the second floor / of the Ambridge Dodge dealer" where they "huddled on a ledge" as the ball hit the pins and "everything exploded in our faces" like Walter Cronkite's Evening News reports of the Vietnam War—mortars landing at supper time ("Setting Pins, 1966").

Winter, Pittsburgh, "sons . . . coming home in boxes" from Vietnam, lay offs, mills closing, and banks calling in loans, it took awhile for "everyone . . . working overtime," piling up money "abstract in the bank" to recognize that history "was right on top of us, / too close to see" ("The History of Steel").

In the black morning of Riviera Beach, South Florida, a seventeen-year-old stockroom boy, thinking of his girlfriend "wrapped in blankets, home," mumbles to himself "past bloody fryer boxes / and through the greasy backdoor smell" of Morrison's Cafeteria. "One more day, he thinks" ("Morrison's 1968").

Hanging tobacco while "straddling the rafters [of a tobacco barn], singing / into the charred roof" and dreaming "of making love," the poet can say, paradoxically, to himself and his buddy Daniel, "this is work" we'd "be lying to claim we want for more than a day. / Lying to say it doesn't feel good here, / getting it done" ("Hanging Tobacco").

Cutting seed stalks from the stems of carrot plants in Gilroy, California, the poet and Daniel sweat "like every other worker / that August, but ours never sank / clean to the roots," and after a month, they "drove away rich, /

drank wine through the Napa Valley" ("Seed Harvest, Gilroy, California").

At the grindstone factory where he "worked the crew that pulled / hot stones from oven racks," the poet listens every day to Vinnie tell him "how to pack five stones / in a box and stencil / the address across the top," instructions worth repeating because this was Vinnie's life "and it had to be more than a kid / could learn in just one morning" ("For the Old Men at the Grindstone Factory").

Then comes "Body Song, Vietnam." The persona, working graves registration, laments bodies "that had barely survived / love and betrayal, birth and baptism." "They came in / like torn dolls, red, gaping holes." The poem's persona just wants "to patch them up" and "send them back to Flint and Gary, to / auto plants and assembly lines, to the girls / whose photos faded in their duffels."

He would prefer to "do the train," an express train coming "through low and fast, steady." He just wants to go "with the rhythm / till you can't get off the track." He wants to believe he had "earned it" ("Harmonica Lesson").

He traversed the country to try and learn how "to live in this world / as if it's the only one," like waiting in the "good green of centerfield" until you hear the crack and "break for the fence, / leap high and backhand one going over," a job well done ("Well Done").

In Part III, the quest turns spiritual, becoming more of a search for meaning, "some land that must live within" ("Letter to Kathy from a Frigate at Sea"). The poet picks up a voice "faint, crackly, distant," coming in "across miles of fields and memories" ("Discourse"). This could be the voice of *longing*, the voice of *love* . . . for the seashell salesman, his "dashboard Jesus, and Mary / in a shell grotto, green light flowing by his daughter's bed" leading him home nights ("Seashell Salesman"); love for "a cycle of cicada song / rising from the creek, rattling / the hardwood leaves, and soaring" ("Meditation on Today's Limit of Pleasure"); for the "New Mount Zion Baptist's / roadside marquee"—"The Holy Ghost is For Everyone" ("Pensacola Street Sunrise"); for a woman, Penelope to his Odysseus now ready to return home, "little left to prove with this wandering" ("Letter to Kathy from a Frigate at Sea"). The poet is ready to forget "that other life. / It's just a hole between the last time I saw you / and now, this life, our life" ("The Geography of Desire").

Part IV continues the poet's cartography of desire, now in Florida "under this rare / historical sky" ("Confluence"), "instant Floridians" ("Leaving Home, Pittsburgh, 1966"). "Everywhere we see the strange world / we have to learn to live" ("Leaving Home, Pittsburgh, 1966"). This is a fecund land—sea creatures mating in the shallows, turtles come ashore to deposit eggs, "alligators / floating the slow black river," "cabbage palms," and "rounded orange trees" ("Orange Nights, Cold Stars"). The beach is "a stretch of sand" where strangers fumble "at buttons, snaps and zippers," exploring the shores of each other's bodies ("Juno Beach and the Sea Turtle"), "driven like pioneers toward some end, / something we could mistake for love" ("Horseshoe Crabs Mating at Carrabelle Beach"). The poet wants "to see everything like a biologist, / an anthropologist of the heart" ("Juno Beach and the Sea Turtle"). He wants his world to begin again ("The Breathers, St. Mark's Lighthouse") like the Ohio River, once "rank / with oil," now "coming back to river once again. / In the cold ruin of the Ohio's banks / muskies swim the secret paths below" ("Even the Ohio Can Change").

In the concluding section of this quest, "what should be a lost mariner's tale / becomes a journey to the spring of provenance" ("On the Water of My Mistakes"). His wife's love is the poet's salvation: "Love is a great, soft, shining buoy / and the end of the rope is in her hand" ("On the Water of My Mistakes"). Now he knows "the water of my mistakes / floats me home to the land / that was always shining" ("On the Water of My Mistakes"), "the unseen geography of our lives" ("Proving Lake Okeechobee").

In "A Thousand Miles from Della Rose," the final poem in the sequence, the poet/persona has returned to Pennsylvania. He thinks about his losses: his mother, the *Rose* of his daughter's name; the Ohio River valley that "made" him; the "dark cold mills, singing / of our lost gods"; "forge, foundry, / furnace, the black smoke and slag." His home, now, is Florida with his wife and their daughter. He has traded "steel for flowers." The Ohio still flows through his old life, but he will not look back at where he has been. He has found the headwaters of a new river. He is going home to his wife and daughter.

Robert Fink
Abilene, 2001

I

Legend

He came from a land that didn't need words.
Fire singed the sky, soot and ash
settled on the tongue. Speech
was furred and superfluous.
He grew older and left, crisscrossed
America, sat silent and stranger
in the loud seats of cars. Salesman
and truck driver wove their special language,
piston-driven to talk and brood.
He listened and thought his shadow
saved them from their lost dreams.
Throughout his land he became legend,
Buck's boy who never talked. No one
at the Legion or VFW; no one
at the hundred Bohunk and Italian bars;
no one at J&L, Armco, Coppers,
Phoenix Glass, or American Bridge;
no cops; no railroad dicks;
no coaches named Maccalini
ever heard him speak. He saved it.
It's for you and you haven't come yet.

The Poem in the River

1.

Someday you'll find this.
You're walking down by the old pump house
on the point where we fished for cats and carp
and you see this bottle wedged among stones
and wood. Gasoline blues and yellows
catch your eye; the bottle shoots its
oily light at you like an old friend. Listen.
The man who shot your father was found
not far from here. He raped a woman
and then fell asleep in her bed.
I didn't ask for this. It was always coming.
Pick up the bottle. Take it home.

2.

The river riddles our blood.
Barges ride low, anthracite shines
in the rare sun. Slag falls
down the bank like lava—red, bubbling,
hissing into the gray water. Winter days
when the wind scrapes the sky clean, you can stand
on this bridge and almost see the shore
where the Ohio bends west and begins its run
for the Mississippi. You might think of a flatboat
and chant the names of towns that take you
away from here—Cincinnatti, Paducah, Cairo, New Orleans.
But you might just see this bridge for what it is,
a cable between Jones and Laughlin's fires

and the houses that ride the hillsides,
and know that three times a day
it comes to its life: a swing shift string
of dirty cars full of men and women with long last names—
names full of impossible vowels and consonants—
waiting for the light to turn green
and send them into the streets of Ambridge,
Aliquippa. Home, to sleep, to eat, to get up,
to go to work again.

3.

If you leave here alive
your memory fades from their eyes.
My favorite graveyard sleeps
on a bluff over the river.
No one's been buried here in years
but the borough still cuts the grass,
tends the graves in that meager way
any paid body cares for the souls
in its charge. I like to come here
and rest my head against Mary Ehman's stone,
look down over the tracks and watch the river
slide past the mill. I look for details,
a scene I missed, and remember my grandfather's story
about sleigh rides across the frozen sheet
of river. I try to remember Crow Island
that I saw every day and then it was gone.
The far edge of the river filled with slag
and stone until the island was riverbank

and the bank was a furnace. The names
on these stones are German; the first
settlers here were mystic, communal,
rich, and celibate. Walking, singing contradictions
who died out and sold the land to steel.
We are their children, in our way;
our world began here and it's come to this—
the mill burning the black sky, cranking, screeching, hissing
through the night. The beauty
of the fire and light dancing on slick water.

4.

The Dream

We were sitting on the old locks,
and the golden carp that swim so slowly
there, as if they were ornaments
in an Asian garden, turned to muskies.
The water was suddenly blue and cold. We waded in.
The river rolled between our legs; we grabbed for fins,
but they swam toward the channel, deep water,
dredged for barges. Somehow,
you grabbed one, locked your fingers
in its gills, yanked him out of the water.
As he fought the air's wrong elements
his tail arced and slapped your belly,
the sound was loud as a pistol's clap.
Blood ran down your arms. I cried out,
lost my step and fell against the riprap wall.

Your father was bleeding as you held him,
gutted, open for all the world to see.

5.

I read the police report. A good-looking young man,
three-piece suit, sawed-off shotgun.
A blast like that in your father's little house
seems like it would blow the walls down,
make the air shudder like freight cars ramming
in the yard. I see blood seeping
out of your house, staining the snow red
on the porch steps, and your father against the far wall,
staring at the door kicked off its hinges.
Remember the night we broke into State Street school,
ate the ravioli and fruit cocktail,
found the tape deck and recorded ourselves singing folk
    songs?
You thought that was crime. You told Sammy,
turned yourself in. A man's supposed to die
slow here. Forty years in the mill. Soot
in the attic settling in your lungs. Quiet.

6.

The poem is in the river.
The wind slashing across the bridge
blows straight into my face.
I scream my hate for this valley,
but it comes back love. I've been in Ambridge,

drinking my way through bars, looking
for a woman who could see
that if she took me home, drunk
and hating the fire in the sky,
she'd get all the years of soot and dying,
slag and shift whistles, in one hard night.
It took a lot of bars,
but I found her near the end of Merchant Street.
I could see the whole thing
glistening below her throat.
I told her everything: about the shotgun,
the soot, you and the bottle. She laughed and said
the soot is our life; the river what we love.
I tried to hate, but it passed through her
into the German fields, Mary Ehman's grass plot.
She was what I can't shake off. Why I go home.
I'm leaning over the rail. In an hour
they will leave their dark houses in streams,
make their way down the hills and along
the river's banks, headlights pushing
into the thick air. It wouldn't do
to be standing here, to say there is a poem
in this bottle for our fathers
and I'm throwing it off the bridge.

Ohio River Sunday

I liked to say
et cum spiritu tuo
and imagine
tutuos echoing as they
escaped the drab brick walls
of St. John's church, rising
like doves in the pictures,
like the Holy Spirit,
and then, realizing
they were free, taking off
up river, going North
where the sky was clean
and white barns dotted green fields.

I liked the tangible church,
the archeological smoothness of the cold,
rubbed pew. The way the palms
of Slovak workers darkened and shined
the wood as they shuffled to communion.
I liked to kneel in the shiny indentations.
A boy could wander along,
watching the rosary beads slide

through his grandmother's liver-spotted hands
until he was lost in his missal
and the strange-tongued prayers.

I was jarred back to my hard wood
when the lambs were swept on a tide
toward the altar to receive the host.
I sat exposed, a boy who'd missed confession.
I wanted to go to the rail like some glowing bird,
pluck the wafer and see if behind my closed eyes
whispered prayers rose toward the sooty windows,
joined the doves, and drifted off to God.

Gasoline

Ten feet above the Boat Dock Bar
a freight highballing down
a clear track through the yard
shatters the air. Shot glasses
shake on the shelf and the jukebox drowns.
On the porch, too many beers gone,
Chuck declares our transient love
for this sodden river. Mill fires
flash iron flowers. Motorboats
bob in slips; oil slicks ring
their hulls. We dance
out and down the dock
singing Jake's favorite blues.

She's got eyes like crystal water
lips like cherry wine
a body like fine brandy
and a soul like turpentine.
O mama, you treat your daddy so damn mean
when I ask for water, you bring me gasoline

Barge lights ghost upriver
and disappear. One old couch
hosts this reunion. We come back
as much as we can stand it. Talk
about the old bars closed.
The Bridgewater, the Friendly.
Talk about the next road
out. We know we were lucky
to be born here. Lucky
we learned to leave.
Any time. Any weather. Any direction.

The Wall

This is the topo map of the world
we have half-survived, the ground
we bring the bodies home to. We walk
in our funeral passion, shoulder to shoulder,
year after year, until the dead soar above us
and we sink into the rock, meld
with fifty thousand etched names.

I do not know that I came for this—
1967, Panel 8, 32 lines down. I ask
the ranger for pencil and paper and as I rub
he blooms under my hand. Suddenly,
too fast for my sense of history, I hold
Larry W. Pierce's gray block memory and see
him, awkward, slow and fat, almost blind
with his thick glasses, taped frames
sliding down his nose.

I see him struggling to be like us,
to have the same small grace we
would throw into his face every day. Larry
who fell trying to run the bases,
who could not hide in hide and seek,
whose body seemed to radiate where he was,
whose feet could not sneak back to the safety
of home, where we stood "in free," waiting
for him to be it again.

Late November, the Coming of Winter
At State Street Elementary School

Down on State Street
the locust and maple trees,
even the one incongruous pear,
would have lost their leaves
and shone wet-black
against the mill's gray sky.
The river would be the color
of cold steel; the terraced hill
between our school and the bare trees,
brown. That much is easy.
Late November, 1963, western Pennsylvania.

This I swear I remember: we are
at recess, playing football
around and through those not in the game.
Someone hooks around the girls jumping
rope, goes long and I can throw
the midget football from one end
of the playground to the other.

Most of us would have sat silent, awkward
as students who hadn't done their homework,
as Mr. Bruno fumbled through his explanation.
Maybe he tried to remind us of history,
Lincoln and Booth, Garfield and the man with the foreign
name. But I know that they sent us home

on a sudden holiday and we walked up the steep hill
to Anthony Wayne Terrace Public Housing.
The Mickey twins, Timmy or Tommy
maybe one of them was crying
as he stumbled up the steps beside Walt's Grocery.

Billy Egidi and I might have talked about it,
tried to comfort or scare each other,
but probably we just cut
through the woods, wove our way through
fallen leaves as the sky turned pink
and the sun fell behind
the Ohio's escarpment.

Creeley Cursing in Church

Fuck, he said.
Why not? Where I come from *God damn it*
was a curse on every sooty thing
in our graveyard-shift life.
God heard them mutter *damn*
as they crowded the bus stop, winter
cracking off the river.
God heard men cry *shit*
when the hammer busts a thumb.
Heard them scream *oh christ*
when the saw blade
ripped through sweet skin.
Heard *oh jesus, mary*[1]
mother of god,
when Louie fell
into the smelter and left
his strange mark on every beam
poured that week.

The Spring in Tevebaugh Hollow

It was across the creek
and the tar road, shadow cut
by rock and locust tree.
In the hollow's rim, caves bloomed.
Fossils etched dark stone. In old fields,
untended, grown thick with blackberry and sumac,
rusted oil pumps posed like herons—
silent, considering Rockefeller, Flagler,
culture's quick slide to obsolescence.

People came like pilgrims, filling jugs
with water sweeter than any borough pipes hauled.
On breaks between pick-up games
we ringed the stone grotto, slurped from cupped hands
and replayed Fenchak's homerun,
laughed at Ralph pumping around the bases
as the right fielder chased the ball
into the Queen Anne's lace of our fenceless field.

That summer, our fathers' and grandfathers'
jobs, the lives they believed in,
waited for us to finish our games
and walk through the fences of Armco,
American Bridge, Jones and Laughlin.
All we knew then was life began there, at Tevebaugh,
when every last one of us was alive,
and the future hung like a slow curve,
seams fat as tracks on a railroad crossing sign.

Caterpillars

In crab apple trees white cocoons
hang like cotton candy.
My father's kerosene torch
touches the first fine web with fire.
From the porch I smell the burning
and hear the caterpillars crackle.
He wants me beside him,
but I close my eyes and see flames
leap from tree to tree,
jump the street and suddenly
the neighborhood burns like a village
on the six o'clock news. We are running—
even fat Mrs. Fabinich—licked with fire
like Holy Ghosts. In the ashes
of our tract houses
I stand with the neighbors
muttering curses in Polish.
This time you have gone too far.

The Candles at Margaret Mary Catholic Church

The body parts of 132 souls
are red flagged with baggage tickets.
I used to sit and stare at that ridge
where the pale sun fell early
and wonder what was beyond it. Later
when I learned about Ohio, Indiana,
the prairies and the mountains west,
I still couldn't believe that my hill,
backdrop to barges working the river,
was the wall between me and the world.

Now, just over the ridge in Hopewell Township
where high, drunk, or both I drove too fast
home from Pudi's or Chuck's, where it was
always too dark when I searched for my turn
down the hill to the lights of the river—
Coraopolis, Sewickley, Aliquippa—
America knows Beaver County now. Wire stories
find these hills domestic: rolling *like the folds
of a blanket on an unmade bed.* They
don't mention the abandoned mills

that were our daily bread, just airplane parts,
flight logs, *deployed thrust reversers,* legs and arms,
tangled in a ravine of hemlock.

Early September, the hills are still green.
From 6000 feet you can see Pittsburgh downriver,
the Ohio under your wing, and the land rolling
east dotted with silos and barns.
I could be on this plane flying home,
on a path animated on the nightly news,
and when we fall faster than three rattled Hail Marys,
I would know well what earth rushes to claim me.

How the Streets in Front of Kaufmann's Department Store Tell Me I Am Home

For years I have been lost. Some nights I have known it
    as I looked out at whatever moon hung
over the wrong trees, watched as too bright stars
    glimmered in a too clear sky.
Other nights, sometimes for months or years I have thought
    I was home because the land

had grown familiar, because live oak and loblolly,
    palmetto or magnolia had begun to speak to me
in a tongue I understood. I said *I live here,* and the dark angels
    that flitted about my shoulders, tickling my ears
with their doubts, fell silent in front of the beauty of azaleas,
    the mystery of camellias.

But today I see that I have been gone these many years.
    Three days after snow, little rivers of cinder water
run in the gutters, ridges of plowed snow blacken
    where glass and steel cut off the sun. And
in front of Kaufmann's, in the great windows where mannequins
    show us what we *could* look like

my people—men and women wrapped in gray or brown coats,
        carrying plastic bags, lunch boxes, briefcases, staring
straight ahead or into the past—walk the lunchtime sidewalks.
        We dodge each other, snow and ice and running water.
I'm drawn to the deli across the street, to pastrami and Iron City,
        where everyone eating big sandwiches is big

and thick, and their voices sing *Pittsburgh* when they say *Iron.*
        On the street again in the dark canyon
of Grant Street, I head for the river and Mt. Washington rising
        on its far shore. My eyes climb the tracks
on the incline, its red car inching skyward like a bucket of coal
        winched up a cliff. The Monongahela

is running high and fast, spring snow
        runoff carrying trees, beds, chairs,
and trash toward the Ohio, and I know I am home
        because from here on this bridge
I can see the Allegheny's muddy mountain water
        merge with this gray to birth the Ohio. No headwaters,

no springs rising in a quiet swamp of cattails, the Ohio
      rolls full bore past Neville Island's
abandoned steel plants, past the silence of American Bridge,
      past the gravel slab that was once Jones & Laughlin,
past my bedroom window that once saw the fire, smoke,
      and ash of three shifts a day, a whole valley working,

living mill lives. From here, because I know that I am home,
      I can see twenty-five miles downriver as it bends
at Beaver and runs west to East Liverpool,where
      my grandfather bought his shoes and worked his first job,
and then turns south for Martin's Ferry, James Wright, and Wheeling.
      I am home today, all of us

standing in front of Kaufmann's windows, waiting
for the light to change, together at last.

II

Setting Pins, 1966

Billy and I got a job
on the edge of extinction,
setting pins in an alley
on the second floor
over the Ambridge Dodge dealer.
We huddled on a ledge
and watched the ball roll
down the lane, spin backwards
and turn into its hook.
It seemed to slow just before
everything exploded in our faces.
All I could do was tuck my head
in my arms, hope I didn't get hit,
and then jump out to sort the dead
from survivors. Windows behind us
gaped ragged black holes from pins
that had rocketed into the mill town night.
We set it up again and waited.
Cold wind seeped down our backs.

In a few weeks our fathers grew tired
of driving into the night to get us,
tired of our walking dazed through school.
They said it was over and brought us home.
We could eat supper again in front of the TV.
Cronkite had our old job, sorting.
Each night, mortars shattered the air.
Bombs drifted like feathers
to the checkered earth below.

The History of Steel

In winter we wore thick coats
and hats with ear muffs folded down,
snapped under our chins.
We carried black lunch boxes
to the bus stop and waited
in the sharp, wet wind.
Others drove soot-streaked
made-in-America cars and jammed
traffic three times a day.

When everyone was working overtime
and money was thick as air,
sons started coming home in boxes.
Few saw how high prices had climbed.
Then the lay-offs began.
Union reps mumbled patience
and it was easy enough to take.

Benefits were good. Money
that had come so fast, before
anyone learned how to spend it,
sat abstract in the bank.
People said we were doing OK.
Had time to panel the basement,
go fishing up at the lake.

History was right on top of us,
too close to see. Mills closed.
Banks called in loans, and markets
filled with grown men, bagging
groceries, shopping while their wives

worked. When time is all you have
yards are manicured, cars repaired,
houses painted one last bright time.

They told us the Japanese did it
so we threw rocks at foreign cars.
Up in the Pittsburgh office
they bought oil companies
and real estate. We didn't
understand business either.

For years they chanted *recovery.*
It sounded like a prayer. We waited.
When they said clear out your locker
and the For Sale sign went up,
        we understood.

Last month someone voted Pittsburgh
the best city to live in. Someone
working somewhere else. Things
are easier to see in this new light.
History is our life now.
Like scholars, we are the subjects
of our own idle debate.

Morrison's, 1968

In the Riviera Beach black morning
where the secret cold is hidden
from tourists, where only workers
and fishermen on an early mackerel tide
know freezing is a South Florida word,
a 17-year-old boy walks to the back door
of Morrison's Cafeteria. Rats scatter
as he mumbles past bloody fryer boxes
and through the greasy backdoor smell.
He hits the lights at the breaker box,
stumbles to the bathroom for starched
white work pants. Ten more minutes
he figures he can steal,
so he sits on the toilet and leans his head
on the sticky wall. Chef Narville bangs
the door as he walks down the hall
to change in the black bathroom.
Saturday begins. This is it.
In another world the sun will rise
over the sea. Lovers and drunks sleep
in the sand. His girlfriend is wrapped
in blankets, home. Her touch
still on his hands, but even that
won't save him, so he struggles out
to the stockroom. One more day, he thinks.

Hanging Tobacco

Blue gauze air, laces of light
bend through the barn. The peaked ceiling
smells like an old bar, walls soaked
in Camels. It hits your tongue
like your Grandfather's stained fingers.
He hugs your neck, his hand you taste
and keep.

But this is work. Love maybe,
the sweat and hurt, the one time
for the hell of it. Calves and thighs flicker.
Hands brown and sticky, face like a dustbowl
Okie's, this is a feeling
we'd be lying to claim we want for more than a day.
Lying to say it doesn't feel good here,
getting it done.

Seventh wagon. Leaves fat as Ohio catfish.
Tired of jerking lead-heavy sticks
from my ankles to the beams overhead,
I yell down to Daniel on the flatbed:
Sing. It's hot up here.

> *Chew my 'baccer, spit my juice*
> *Gonna love my baby till it ain't no use*
> *An' ho, ho baby, take a whiff on me.*

I'm straddling the rafters singing
into the charred roof. The songs hang

in the thick air and curl around the barn.
Down below the song turns bawdy.
My hips remember a better ache, a better reason
to push for the ceiling. If there's a wrong time
to dream of making love, this is it.
Thirty feet up in a tobacco barn. No net.

They say you get high on your first smoke.
In the last six hours I've sucked down
every Pall Mall since Truman beat Dewey.
Her red river hair flows over my hands,
eyes blue as the late sky outside
the slatted vents of the barn.
This is a dangerous business.

Last spike hung. Climb down the wall
like a gray spider, stretch from beam
to beam to pull the muscles long again.
Whiskey cuts the stale air in our throats.
Back of the truck we're belting Leadbelly's blues—
You take Sally an I'll take Sue—
down the red clay roads home.

Seed Harvest, Gilroy, California

for Daniel

Each cold morning we drove
down from Coyote Lake in a fog.
By nine we'd thrown off
our sweatshirts. Seed crowns
danced in rolling heat waves.
We tied burlap sacks to our belts
and cut seed stalks from stems
as we waded through waist high
carrot plants. Dust clung
to our arms and hands, smoothed
to an ooze that streaked cracks of skin,
became thin brown bracelets around wrists,
spider webs etching the insides
of our elbows.

The noon sun burned
behind a mean smear of haze.
We moved like ants
dragging beetles through dirt.
Along the highway to Los Banos
workers stooped to green leaves
and pulled red globes from a dirt heaven.
Kerchiefed heads and straw hats
moved through tomato fields

like Millet's peasants.
McCormick's vats steeped the valley
with an odor of pizza.

We sweated like every other worker
that August, but ours never sank
clean to the roots. We picked seed
while carrots and onions rotted
in the earth. Special migrants, white.
A letter of introduction from your father
bought us poverty like a souvenir
from a Monterrey gift shop.

In the evening we stood
under the cold hose and rinsed
off a day's dirt. We climbed
into the van and the hot wind blew
us clean. On the mountain we stopped
for a beer, laughed with the fat bartender,
and held iced mugs to our cheeks.
After a month we drove away rich,
drank wine through the Napa Valley.
Names of towns rolled like rain
across the map. Petaluma.
Mendocino. Albion.

For the Old Men at the Grindstone Factory

Vinnie told me every day
how to pack five stones
in a box and stencil
the address across the top
because it was his life
and it had to be more than a kid
could learn in just one morning.

Skinny Billy's voice squeaked
when he asked, "Where you goin' next?"
He knew he would bind grinding wheels
until tomorrow was flat and forgotten.

I worked the crew that pulled
hot stones from oven racks.
Silica burned under asbestos gloves,
scorched our cheeks
because the foreman would not wait
for a rack to cool.
Red welts bloomed
on the lifers' faces
like ID cards.

At quitting time we ran
for the time clock
and bunched like school children
cramming through the door.
In the Somerville winter

we huddled in metal shelters
for the bus to home or bar.
Tool and die plants in Gary,
Buffalo, and Cleveland
waited for our day's work.

Body Song, Vietnam

The bodies should have been marked
fragile. Bodies that had barely survived
love and betrayal, birth and baptism,
were not ready for war. They came in
like torn dolls, red, gaping holes.
I just wanted to patch them up,
send them back to Flint and Gary,
to auto plants and assembly lines, to the girls
whose photos faded in their duffels.

At first, I tried to ignore the war
and find reminders of the world outside:
a scar on the cheek from a fishing hook,
cleat mark from a sliding runner,
nose bent by a careless elbow. They were like streets
I knew, windows I had looked through summer nights
and wondered who played the piano,
who cut the flowers that were always
fresh in the crystal vase.

But that was when I was new. The words
of the world went away and I named things
for what I saw. The song changed.
One had a hole where his mother was.
Rice paddy mud where he thought he might go
to college. One held his stomach
on his thigh like a gift, and one's arm

is still flying in the mine's
red wind. Another just stared
at the oily sky.

One night in the Queen Bee I heard Khanh Ly
sing "Love Song of a Woman Driven Mad
By the War." We joined in on
I had a lover who died . . .

Harmonica Lesson

Don't showboat if you can't do the train.
Go down by the tracks
and wait. Let the freights go.
They're good for blues, but you're
too new for that. Express trains
come through low and fast, steady
as a good bass man. Stay down
near the two-hole. Go with the rhythm
till you can't get off the track.
Like this. Tight-belly staccato,
hands cutting and freeing the air,
one hard-held bottom line. Play between
trains. Keep the wheels in mind.
Catch the next one and play all night.
In the morning try the whistle. You've earned it.
It should sound like Kansas.

Well Done

for Bob Coles

I want to say to a world that feels
with reason it has little chance, well done.
Richard Hugo
"Letter to Mantsch from Havre"

I will not say there is anything good in this,
will not talk of metaphysics
or heaven. You're dead, a bullet between the eyes.
I want to live in this world
as if it's the only one. Live
where the morning moon glides
like a hawk. Walk along the coast
and watch breakers swell like humpbacked whales.
Or maybe just stay home
knowing that the dogwoods will break out singing,
that the sky here couldn't be bluer
for blood or money. Stand in early February
without my shirt, in the good green of centerfield,
hear the crack and break for the fence,
leap high and backhand one going over.

III

Discourse

The ones I like best seem to be
spoken by somebody else, a person
(I'd say voice inside my head, but I
don't like that disembodied wisp
floating free to lodge where it may,
free to come out where it will, at
the hardware store, or the Tripple D grocery
where I'm just buying milk,
and likely to be misunderstood
if suddenly I were rattling off lines
about soot and slag, or even a simple
pastoral iambic about fences
and cows so I say *person*) inside my head
because it's more substantial, a fleshy

full-bodied noun that I imagine
has to use doors like the rest of us
and so will at least knock or make
floorboards creak before he (or she)
comes out to surprise—or in this world—
embarrass me, since I'm not in
a church deep in the piney woods
speaking in tongues, but just poetry, so
the person, he or she (the she is a little
more unnerving, biologically, although a part
of me has sometimes wanted to be a woman,

or at least been sure I was often ashamed to be a man,
though, don't get me wrong,
I could play shortstop and centerfield with the best

of them—them being men, since I
grew up with Roberto Clemente, Willie Mays,
Mickey Mantle and Ernie Banks, back when Banks
was a shortstop hitting forty homers a year, though
I was more of a Dick Groat shortstop: spray hitter, lots
of doubles, no Aparicio with the glove, but dependable)
so the person inside of me—man, woman, or both in some

commingling I'd rather not speculate on here—I can trust
to come mostly when it's appropriate and stay
in the back room when it's not. I remember
being told we had to become vessels
ready to receive, so really it's sort of a cooperative
thing, a symbiotic life we live where the other person
isn't really a parasite leaching off the vast income

of a freshman comp teacher (though I don't know
how this person gets his or her money; I suspect
it's mostly through the kindness of strangers
or the meager largesse of government agencies
giving money for art in a world as odd and specialized
as the Tripple D's Big Buck Contest that
admits many people who think words come in lines,
measured, unmeasured, but formed for arcane and uncertain
purpose). This other person is somewhat dependent
on me—father, husband, teacher, publisher, fisherman,

driver, dog feeder, garden hoer, grass cutter, tree
pruner—to open the door from that back room and let him or her
wander (dressed how?) through the rest of the house
until he or she—let's say she—comes out talking,
and words, not really these, but perhaps some of these,

come out. It's usually near dawn. Trees are just appearing
and I'm alone, except for a dog or two. I usually have
a pencil and I write the words down like a man
glossing the vaguely Babylonian language of a Pentecostal babbler,
or the words of an alien race as they arc across radio wires,
or maybe like the Sunday in Pittsfield, Massachusetts,
where for eight hours Bob Steinem and I
were the only ones waiting for a train
and I picked up the pay phone to slam it down
on the hook to see if a dime would come out
and instead heard Mick Jagger singing
Gimme Shelter, not loud and clear, like a radio,
but faint, crackly, distant, like a voice singing
across miles of fields and memories.

Seashell Salesman

Abalone ashtrays littered with butts.
His life made him nervous—a French Canadian
wandering through the land of Calusa and Tequesta,
driving the two-lane shell roads from Fort Myers
to Vero Beach, his wares rattling in boxes
as he stared across saw grass and swamps
at hammocks nesting against the blue sky.
In the triangle that bordered the Everglades,
to every truck stop and tourist shop shining
in the day's hot sun and swimming in a sea of bugs
the parking lot lights and neon lured home,
he delivered the tourists' proof that they had been here,
and their dollars kept his seven kids in Catholic schools.
His life was strung from Sea Shell City to Monkey Jungle
and the thin line of what he knew about coffee and pie
filled his ledger books. A dashboard Jesus, and Mary
in a shell grotto, green light glowing by his daughter's bed,
led him home nights, late, when the air
was thick with honeysuckle and the banyan
leaves rattled in the offshore breeze.

Meditation on Today's Limit of Pleasure

Sometimes the cicadas come riding in wild
and grow loud in the trees, like a tide
that surges every few seconds.
We could call it a cycle of cicada song
rising from the creek, rattling
the hardwood leaves, and soaring
into the loblollies, until they seem
to take off, each one a jet
engine on full, flying into the sun
and a universe that hovers in the blue
tomorrow, the promise early October
makes. I want to be the man,
the God, the recording engineer
who sits far off in the lost bower of harmonics
turning the knob marked CICADA—turning it
past four, past five, to seven and eight—
and then backing off, somewhere in my heart
the hint of mercy saying *We can't stand anymore.*
This song. This sun. This blue. These cicadas.

Pensacola Street Sunrise

The New Mount Zion Baptist's
roadside marquee
rising from palmetto scrub
advertises
The Holy Ghost is For Everyone.
There were days
when I wanted to see the Holy Ghost.
In my catechism I couldn't tell
if he was a spirit or a dove. I
don't know that we had doves
along the river, but pigeons
I'd seen walking Merchant Street
in Ambridge, perched
on ledges in downtown Pittsburgh, cold
winter pigeons in the lights
of Horne's and Gimbel's Christmas windows.
Never a Holy Ghost, unless
it was in the light of the fires
that scored the river's
steel mill shores. Later
I came to know doves
cooing in live oak trees
a lifetime from the river. I
could take them for holy
but hardly ghosts.

Letter to Kathy from a Frigate at Sea

The ship is dark. Red light echoes
in the passageway. Late, like this,
I feel like I'm the only one awake.
But someone watches faint green radar blips,
spots running lights on the flat horizon.
Green lights starboard, red for port.
I'm sad and I'm eating. Bad habit.
I want you to stop smoking,
but I can't ignore this lonely passion
for sweets. Tonight, chocolate ice cream
and chocolate cream pie. I raided the pantry.
I'd give up midnight snacks to sit
on the back porch and watch the moon
through the live oak leaves. Sentimental
slob I'm becoming. This life is not for me.
Can't sleep at night, can't stay awake
during the day. When I get home
please keep me there. I've little left
to prove with this wandering. I know
all about picking up and leaving, traveling
light, and waking lost. The ship creaks
like a rusty hinge, strains and pops
like a trailer in the wind. The teletype
chatters about my head, and the bulkhead
rumbles as a hatch slams shut below.
Last year, in Wyoming, I thought
the prairie was as far away
as I could get. Brown land,
flat to the mountains, winters frozen,
black and empty as the sea. This afternoon
the ocean was a deeper blue

than mapmakers claim.
I wanted to jump off the fantail
and sink through layer after layer
to some land that must live within.
Let's get together and buy an atlas.
Pick a color to live in. I'll write
from somewhere warm and bright,
and deliver my letters by hand.

To Jennifer, Thinking of Li Po

Now, with you in Seattle,
where cloud and mountain
rise, inseparable
as river and rain,
I ask, as Li Po did
so many times,
when will we meet again?
Mottled light falls green,
shadows fill my backyard.
Your letter crinkles in humid air
as if it came from a time distant
as we are in space.
In the summer sky
the sun runs west,
wild flowers dot the roadside.
So far. Everything that is this land
rolls between us.
A thousand exit ramps.
The last lights of towns
that flicker like ships at sea.
Make your life new. Listen.
Li Po stands, moon rising above
Puget Sound, and sings for you now.
The headlands run to the sea,
humped, in starlight,
like loaves of bread, like whales.

The Geography of Desire

If you insist on history
it was Cambridge, 1977. The door
of your flat closed and you disappeared
into the life you thought yours. I walked
streets caked with the winter's last snow.
Spring came that night, though there was little
reason to notice. Nothing to believe.

For years I made you every dark-haired woman
in the streets of Montreal, a bar
in St. Croix. I carried you with me
until now, the moment when our lives
break loose, like sailboats slipping
their moorings.

For years I have practiced stealing you.
Those nights when you dreamed
of flying over a land green with magnolia
and water oak, when you woke damp,
sea air on your neck, when,
for two days, every time you closed your eyes

you saw the Atlantic, I did that.
Those splitshot seconds when you turned
a corner, and everything danced, then settled,

you were living on the border.
I've honed desire beyond time and space

and bent geography into a New World.
This cartography of the heart
is stronger than any map that says Tucson,
any phonebook that says Calle Madrid.

Forget that other life.
It's just a hole between the last time I saw you
and now, this life, our life.

IV

Leaving Home, Pittsburgh 1966

From the gray sky and the gray river,
we come in one day to the New World.
Though passage is no longer arduous and slow,
its displacement is sudden and complete.
The plane lifts into cold January,
and the new year finds us becoming something
we don't understand. In high sun, sharp sky,
we stand on a bleached concrete runway
and wobble in the overwhelming light
to a small white terminal.
We are instant Floridians, squinting
as we turn and see nothing but sky
and thin palms rising from the flat land.
Our lives change in a hurry,
the way immigrants crossed
the sea, changed names and remembered
when they looked at photos,
at old letters, that their lives before
were lived at a different speed
in a different language.
The next morning we wake, forget
our way, our geography,
and are scared again by the light,
the orange trees shining in the yard,
the talk of alligators in the canal.
Everywhere we see the strange world
we have to learn to live. Soon
our tongues are making long vowels,
slowing, warming to our task.

Juno Beach and the Sea Turtle

Old enough to sense the confusion
of the sacred and the profane,
I'm sprawled in the Juno Beach sand
as the moon pools its light on the surf,
and June pulls us all to the shore. We
have come from a bar on US 1, a way station
where migratory tourists greet
the locals. This night we trekked
to a stretch of sand where bodies
and blankets tangle in a dance, mate
in a ritual our singular need fills
with passion. I was there staking
some kind of territory, pulling
at the tight jeans of a woman
who had journeyed long from Akron
to find this beach, this stranger.
Less sense of purpose than geese,
we fumbled at buttons, snaps and zippers
endured sand fleas feasting on our soft flesh
because something that no one explains
called us to explore
the shores of our bodies.

In the roar of surf and skin
I almost didn't hear behind me
the grunting, like an old woman
lugging family laundry. I turned
and saw the loggerhead, slugging
through the high tide wrack of weeds,
bogging down in sugar sand.
She too was called by June,

by the moon, maybe by the lack
of cops and city lights
as she entered our world from the ocean
we thought backdrop, dwarfed
our curious passion, brought me up
short, so to speak. I sat
on our blanket, rapt, as she dug
and grunted each egg into the sand.
I wanted to see everything like a biologist,
an anthropologist of the heart.

   She went slowly back to the sea,
less dramatic than her coming ashore,
less awkward than our parting. With forgotten
names, we climbed the dunes and she dropped me
off at a 7-11, where the light of neon beer signs
glanced off the hoods of cars.

Horseshoe Crabs
Mating at Carrabelle Beach

Through shallow water
warm as a bath,
they swam locked together
like elaborate buttons.
Large and sharp,
dinosaurs of love and necessity.

Nothing pretty in their mating
to move us to wonder
at the ways of the moon,
its intimate currents of desire.

Creatures of whatever god,
these armored mines resist
tenderness, the sloppy thought
of romance and the sea.

I wanted trout,
not rutting crabs blindly knocking
against my shins. In the dirty water

I danced around each piggybacked couple
that swam in a line straight west,
driven like pioneers toward some end,
something we could mistake for love.

Orange Nights, Cold Stars

        Hippies with money
were buying subdivided orange groves
out along the Loxahatchee River.
I wanted one, imagined sleeping
in a small white frame house
with a wraparound screened porch.
In the night, oranges would glow
like shallow stars.

        We walk
the old orchards and watch nighthawks
feed on fat mosquitoes. Moonlight
shows us kites and osprey
and glints in raccoon eyes.
All the air smells of oranges.
Cupboards and pantry full of juice.
Bowls of shining globes on every table,
blossoms floating like hyacinths
in blown-glass pools.

        Even the alligators
floating the slow black river
dream of oranges. When
winter's sinking sun fills
the sky with pastel light,
green, rose, violet layered
one upon another, nothing
is left but the near horizon
of cabbage palms, and, of course,
rounded orange trees.

On cold nights
when the air could kill, we light
the smudge pots left in the sheds.
Smoke drifts into our bedroom
through joints, cracks in sills,
jalousies that won't roll tight.
In our dreams the world is a hazy
picnic of orange-glazed chicken,
leeks with orange ginger sauce, orange
ambrosia, orange flan, blood-orange tea.

On the Seaboard tracks,
distant trains lull us to sleep.
Out in the black night
under almost Southern stars, our grove
snuggles and we curl, spooned
under quilts. In our house without heat
we could find the way, like dreamers,
like settlers homesteading acres of dreams.

Fishing the Encampment

Where the Encampment slowed
to wander through a meadow, I stood
in the day's last light
and plopped a fly in a likely pool.
Up the other bank a black bear
shambled through brush. From far away
I thought I could share the river.
I thought of platitudes
like *they're just as scared as you*
and *the worst thing to do is run.*
When it crossed to a sand spit
in the middle of the shallow water,
I thought of greater truths that had failed me
and reeled in my tenuous bait.
Just like life, what I thought I knew
had stuck me with less options
than I needed. When it crossed
to my side I turned and walked
the trail downriver, entered
a narrow ravine where the dark
closed in on me, and saw in my fear
the bear running, grinning like someone
who knows you can shock the faithful
just by turning them around. All bets
were off and I crashed through brush,
leaped logs and rocks. At every turn
when I couldn't see the trail ahead
I saw the bear—great now, blacker
than the night falling—raise his paw
in one simple act that I should have learned
by then about trust, about what you think
you know about life, or love.

The Breathers, St. Mark's Lighthouse

I stand at the point of the oyster bar
where the water darkens and deepens,
begins to turn for the Gulf. This morning
I am early. Light is new and I think
of Mexico. Somewhere south

past clouds that ride the horizon
the Yucatan jabs into the sea.
The tide's almost slack, turning
like a man remembering his keys.

Pelicans splash like stones; snakebirds
on pilings hang their wings out to dry. Crabs
scuttle the brown shell bottom. All the fish
I do not want are alive and hungry today. Every cast
brings pinfish, needlefish, baby cat.

Dolphins tail over turtle grass beds,
roll and hump through the flats.
Water so shallow it will not cover
their broad, gray-green backs.

All four turn toward me, swim
just a few feet off the bar.
I am almost close enough to read
their minds, to put my thoughts
in their great deep eyes.

As they surface I hear them blow
and it sounds like the gasp of a runner
opening his lungs to the rich air.
I listen to them, the breathers.

Where the map says Apalachee Bay,
where Navárez sailed west in his patchwork
ships, our eyes meet; we breathe the same
air. Today, together, we are so old,
the world begins again.

Confluence

While last night
Venus, Mars, and Jupiter
hung inches north
of the sickle moon,
spring-fed Wakulla, newly loosed
from the earth, stars
dancing in its glass water,
sailed through marsh grass,
whispered to the waiting ears
of alligators the ways of limestone,
and the sudden birth of sinkholes;

it joined the St. Marks,
rolling brown as root beer
through clay, sand, and cypress,
the night sky's few lights
flickering in its slow surface,
at San Marcos de Apalachee
and flowed, conjoined
under this rare
historical sky.

Even the Ohio Can Change

The river I grew up on was rank
with oil. Shoreline stones
gleamed slick-blue and nothing
in the river was worth a slug
of scrap metal: carp and catfish,
sick, riddled with chemical blood.

My river was for barges,
owned by US Steel, ARMCO, J&L.
They pumped it full of slag,
dripped and drained oil and gas
through a thousand hidden holes.

Nothing good could come of it
except a living and life,
a whole valley's clinging dream.
The Indians who named it beautiful river
weren't wrong; how could they know
what would come, dark and sooty,
burning the sky, turning the earth
to mud and cinder?

Even in our terrible need
we couldn't kill it and the river
is coming back to river once again.
In the cold ruin of the Ohio's banks
muskies swim the secret paths below.

We grow older, the river younger,
and great fish smash into the air
to swallow a caterpillar
fallen from a willow branch.

Setting the World in Order

for Maloney and Miranda

In your Cambridge winter,
though I couldn't name poetry,
I heard it: wind off the river,

starlings waking in the bare elm.
I went to work—five days a week,
then four, then three, then none

at all. Walking home the last day,
drifting across Harvard Square
like a tourist, was almost as good

as being in love. In Laramie
I sat, six years later
and two thousand miles away,

at a desk by an upstairs window.
The sun climbed into pure sky, lighting
Pole Mountain's Sherman Pass.

Under the gold crowns of cottonwoods
Wyoming waited for winter. I tried my hand
at your work then. My words cut

across the open land, promised
to go somewhere, not turn to dust
and leave us looking back at where we had been.

V

Bamboo

for Joel

Six years ago it was small,
just a few thin shoots
under the bedroom window.
My wife said let it go.
I knew, since my life
has been more tropical than hers,
that soon all we would know
was the green of tall grass
and that someday the Rose of Sharon
deep inside the stand would be lost
like an ancient village
gone back to earth and foliage. Now,
bamboo climbs toward blue heaven
above the peak of our roof.
Each night I hear wind stir the stalks.
In thick summer bamboo grows
closer to the moon. Though we
are poor stewards of our land, our lives,
our dreams, I have learned from the lizards
and beetles who dwell below our screens
what our careless husbandry will bring.
We will wake one morning
to a soft nibbling and look
into the white faces of pandas
come, gentle, hungry, to save us
from our own soft hearts.

A Walk in the Woods

Sun leaves the ground like fall.
Shadows break, flutter windblown.
The son I don't have walks beside me.
I tell him about trees.
The way woods love earth and air,
put up with birds like he must
the other kids in school. I say look,
blue jays bounding from branch
to branch, screeching in the tree's ear,
chasing each other like you do
on the playground. The tree is patient.
It knows in the winter how long the quiet gets.
He looks at me as if I've never had a thing
to do with kids, but he's kind as grass
and won't hurt me. He knows I read
a poem this afternoon and saw a child
fall from the rafters of an old barn.
And he knows that these things
I carry with me—songs, weather, rivers—
brought him into the world like light
playing over pine needles on the sand.

On Missing the First Step on the Moon

That summer I paid no attention
to anything but one girl and the harmonica
I tried to play, accompanying myself
kicking cinders along the black tar road.
A whole day would pass as I hitched north
through Mennonite cornfields
and white farmhouses. My destination
was Pymatuning, a reservoir over dead farms
whose fences and barns fossil the lake bottom
and the gray-bleached trunks of sycamore
and maple pile along the shore like bones.

I knew they were going.
I was no dullard cut off for years
from the space race and the great Sputnik fear.
But when Apollo rose
and circled the white moon,
I sat under a tree
by a pump and watched geese graze
at the lake's edge. I waited
for my girlfriend to sneak from her house
and join the whirling earth I'd found.
That moonnight before the walk
we were in the cornfield stealing baby ears
and I swear I saw a shadow cut across
the white face as it hung over the road to town.
Days later my father asked
if I'd seen them walk on the moon

and I acted as if I didn't know
they were even in the sky.
It made him angry.
We were closer to being even. My life
was one small step after another,
drifting toward a history all my own.

Angels Flying You Home

for Rosemary Campbell (1924-1992)

Once I read you a poem
about Grandpa's dying on a train
and you said it didn't happen
that way. I had trouble explaining
why I couldn't change it, why
I needed that line to run
to the Indiana cornfields,
to the dark-ridged Charleston hills,
and the gun-metal river.

I went romantic in that one,
had pick and shovel ring
and shiver against the frozen earth.
But you went in that same cold time
and now I know the way the world
takes us home: backhoe
bucket rending shale and clay.

The Kanawha flows through Dunbar, ugly,
cold and gray as I wrote it then. Below
Tyler Mountain Memory Gardens,
the two-lane highway Friday nights
clogs with cars, headlights bleed

into the dark and crawl to a dog track
dream, a ticket out of this life
faster than the one that brought you here.

We have commended you to your God
and for these few moments I believe
not in him, but in you believing in Him.
All the angels who have watched over you,
slipshod as their tenure has been, float
in this rainy West Virginia sky.

After we leave, they have one more task.
It's cold. I'm wearing Grandpa's
long gray coat, mud smears my black shoes.
An Irish priest throws a clod of dirt
as slickered workmen lean against the backhoe.
Beside your plot, Grandma and Grandpa,
brass markers long gone green
in the industrial rain, wait.

The Drowned Son

You want the body to rise.
Nine nights and still
you wait. One time
the phone will ring
and it won't be a friend.
As much as you hate
the vision, you want his body
to float home like driftwood
and be found by a fisherman
working the shoreline pockets.
You want the body finally free
from bottom snags—tree stump,
fence post—the remnants
of these flooded farms.

You see him lurch and lose his grip,
fall face first into the lake.
You imagine how he fights his boots
and heavy coat, the night and beer
pulling him down.

Nine days now you hear the lake
chop and slap in your sleep.
It is the sound of your life.

On the Water of My Mistakes

for Marcia

Vaguely deserving my fate,
I knew another chance wouldn't save me.
No reprieve lasts.
I'd fall again. So I let go.
Darkness washed over my head.
Catfish stared at my bubbles
rising involuntarily
like some champagne gig.

But that's not the story that amazes.
No. I've been borne on the water,
floated like lucky Moses
through my bulrushes,
swept like fortunate fishermen
home, even though stars and seabirds
seemed to say goodbye.

That's the miracle. Not cursed,
but blessed. Barely kicking,
what should be a lost mariner's tale
becomes a journey to the spring of provenance.
Love is a great, soft, shining buoy
and the end of the rope is in her hand.
She pulls, and the water of my mistakes
floats me home to the land
that was always shining.
How easy this is.

Proving Lake Okeechobee

for Marcia

We drive below the sod earth rim,
and I promise it's there, just beyond
the cattle grazing grass and nettles—
big water, fish eye green, flat as a pancake,

a great big bowl of faith.
This is not a developer's scheme
on a two-lane highway where acres of muck farms
end at our window in random patches

of cane, yellowing palms, rusted tractors
and shacks. No one's building a city
of false dreams here where what rings
the rim canal is hardly a promise or a dream.

I've seen it, slid down the rocks to the water
while the burning cane fields of Belle Glade,
Clewiston, and South Bay danced around me
and all of the sky filled with smoke. I stood

at its edge and felt it leaning toward Palm Beach
like a gray-flecked tub of water dreaming

of a return to saw grass and Everglade.
I lived in that pink-sugar air drifting toward the beach.

I want you to take my word
that a lake's back there, but too many times
I've promised to see, to change, to care.
So I drive the steep bank, crawl over the locks,

and hang for a moment on the rim. Before us,
only water and sky; then we fall
down the crushed shell road to the lake
and the unseen geography of our lives.

Trying to Get Pregnant, Flying to Iowa

I left you in the blue morning
carrying inside a secret cache
of sperm charged with wending
their way, I want to say, north
because I see you standing there
saying goodbye, and north is always up
on all my maps. And now the sperm
and I journey our separate but similar
ways. It's as if I have left me
with you in some complicated
reproductive conceit, where chromosomes
swim the ovarian sea, called
by your egg to the New World,
their fountain of youth,
cities of gold, Cibola
or Bimini. I hope they can swim
the uncharted seas better
than their progenitor
who sent them forth without
so much as a lesson, a guiding word.
So early and dark this morning
that, barely awake, they had to sail
with last night's orders:
find land, plant a seed, make a baby.
Then we were asleep again
saving minutes until the alarm.
I crawled into the plane
and found myself over the green squares
of Kansas, flying to Iowa,
the heart of the land.

Long Distance Call 3/95

for Marcia

I'm raining in my soul here.
Streetlights wedge through the granite alley
of the William Penn and whatever stone
sits dumb outside my window. You're crying
this morning, lonely, and I want to be home
with you and tell you everything that I have seen
and not seen this week. How the spring hills
were wet brown as a groundhog pelt,
how the Ohio swirled its muddy flood through Sewickley.
How the mills are silent hulks
marking the remnants of a steel town life.

None of this is what you want to hear and nothing
I ever wanted to say. This life
is over here. Our baby grows inside you,
swelling toward May. There's a hotel full of writers
dreaming this dark morning and nothing
will ever be the same. I'll be home tomorrow.
Wait for me in the coffee shop where the pastries
are far too expensive, and the orange juice
costs a mint. I feel a lucky streak coming,
far, far from this river and the plans
they are forging for its long last days.

A Thousand Miles from Della Rose

When little I remember survives
this life will at last be mine.
As I stand in the valley, I know now
I'll have to tell you of our loss.
Your grandmother, the Rose of your name,
is gone. This valley that made me has gone
to another life. The dark cold mills, singing
of our lost gods and their slaughter block of dreams,
line the river like pall bearers. You'll think
I made too much of this, and I'll tell you all too often
of things you'll never see—forge, foundry,
furnace, the black smoke and slag.
Your land is loblolly and magnolia.
No coal barges crawl through your dreams.
We trade steel for flowers.
You are my new river.

Selected by Robert Fink, *Setting the World in Order* is the tenth winner of the Walt McDonald First-Book Competition in Poetry. The Competition is supported generously through donated subscriptions from *The American Scholar, The Atlantic Monthly, The Georgia Review, Gulf Coast, The Hudson Review, The Massachusetts Review, Poetry, Shenandoah,* and *The Southern Review.*